Popularly Divine Deep In Our Spine

by
Fathy Elsherif

Vol. 1

ISBN: 0692348018
ISBN-13: 978-0692348017

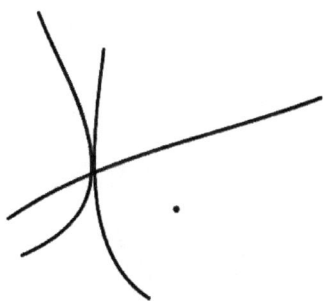

Experimentalists. Theorists.
Clipped wings
Scoped plans of frustration
A lion raised on bitter lioness' biting punishments raises a subdued
wingless dove in a loving desperation for a cub
Or a saccadic toothless shark
Or a junkie feens on needle-less syringes
Or a bald fat fuck salivates on short-order hallow high-heeled magazine
actresses of deceit
Infinite-distance travel on static cartwheels
Nightly unfruitful reflections on soul-sucking afflictions
Self-inflicted cowardice, incompetence, and reaffirmed inaction
Glory's fleeting
Gratitude is cheating
Grate on this

How do you enjoy the ride
How do you observe and keep quiet
Do you know we're automatons
Do you know we're marked
The fleeting moments define time
Neither you nor I will be twice
What we see in the sky now
Was already burnt before our time
Shining stars living in the past
Burning bright to light old paths
We assimilate the brevity of it all
Yet go about it twirling in a dance hall

A friend or foe, confidant or tattler
Your uninformed achromic neologism
Your own archaic-sounding adjectives
None to my character's quality
All is the penultimate of the truth
All is the antonyms of validity
Embroiled I'm not but aim to decimate
Defective attempts at adjective lapidary
None construes antiquated descriptions
None construes with literate accuracy
None of any can compare mine
To my contemporaries' or bygones'
Or evenhandedly classify
Whose is or whose isn't
Still you do with unearned liberties
And paste assertions onto mine
Oozing with grand fallacious judgments
I despise descriptive anthropo-adjectives
My head twists excruciatingly
At nescient blatherskites
Flaunters of grandiose frippery black robes
Blabbers in fabricated courtrooms
Neither you, nor them
Not even the sun
O *mi propia madre*
Knows my ubac
From my adret

It's two forty-four and I've got a mirror, pen, paper and a second language to write in with the talent of an abecedarian and thirty six years of vapor with nothing to show but a ride, a drink, and a light, each from a different person in a nine story building with an edge not for climbing but dips, pits, and pools yet none are made to jump in except when feelings get hurt of people's, pets', and plants' by a galoot's narrowband yet anytime when at loss it don't feel different, except a dream of a hyperlink to a life of learning and leisure that yearns for no process, pattern, or reason but come off like a nidificating geep eternally rooted deep in purgatory as it be neither goat nor sheep with a persistent dream of a lambent woman who's in love with broods by a definite scaramouch who's spiraling in constant hebdomadal life plans of this and that but end with "can't" which elevates anger at the nonsense while this itself makes no sense outside of a game-field with rewards and penalties for some made up sedentary with books in bags and passport stamps and the tilt of my screen capturing secret plans bound in discreet while reminding me of the romantic melodies that massaged my ears, now how them neon lights' bombardment fucking desecrate, and while my own ears sometimes can't believe what comes out of my mouth, my perspective is my prerogative and all else is useless additive.

I remember the time when I was young I scaled her fence all in suspense she was my bingo all dressed in pink like a flamingo I roamed her house in garden city like a li'l mouse under her balcony I played my guitar all the way up to my two only fans raised their hands threw their beer cans my strumming disband I smothered myself in hopes and dreams as I started drownin' in my excess psilocybin when I walked many miles when I was young those peaceful times now I'm high-strung I'm a singing mime so now I hide by my bedside by my nightlight like a deserter like a parasite (here we go... once a-gain. at the window... way out of turn) his chickasaw cigarette hangs from his mouth and paints a silhouette while sleeping on the couch wakes up one morning screams "it was not me I did not decide!" to be ill-named in magazine stains or live in tales by Mark Twain he cries so loud shouts out "mayday!" but to his dismay his candles 're out "confused" he says like orphans in wombs and life-filled tombs like warlords of peace and high-rise catacombs so I follow drum beats heed the pain pleas smash oars in waters like dreams on screens I bide my time through free verse lines find Washington armies livin' in despair with hate 'n stymies on flat-tire wheelchairs and love on psilocybin when no-one's whinin' and no-one's aware I came back to you with my own windmill cover you in pongee but he wouldn't say you were his wife I didn't even know he was alive I decided to stay until you called me and said "hey, you should be free" why you betray and when I tried to call you in to watch me try all my new things said you were busy answering fan letters but that's not true you're now a cribber a snake of leather a mouse a critter a girl named weather so irregular your place's now nether like fossils in stones like marrow in bones like salt in oceans like a dead reborn while now I am the man I can.

Death of a friend, death was her end, death in music, arts in lies
Why must one be judged malcontent because often pried
The majority surrounded she and me were lethargic automatons
Chased to the edge on a finite timeline by indigenous squid on us prawns
I wouldn't forgive in the name of nil
Fugazie & schemes & lies and daydreams & nothing is what it seems
Your face is smeared with smirks and sly
Your fake tears won't erase your grimy deeds
Nor will heed your prayers against exposure fears
Her memories fade but your actions remain
Your story be scorned all through your deep sleep
Now my old hopes and dreams are ruined by what you made real
And yesterday's plan is only good to slam
I get lost, lost in dreams of flowers in fields and her hazel eyes
And fall back in dreams when my sight meets yours
In dreams of flowers in fields and her hazel eyes
Where there once was a warm spring of a friend's embrace turned into icy spikes
Where there once was a safe nest is now straws with worms and thorns
Under it all are promises and pain and time missing
Death you birthed is the death of the end, death in music, arts and stories of lies, and my friend's hazel eyes

People talk of gender types
Some discuss homicides
Minutiae hell on the news
With Dead suns
In my Shoes

Taking my soul out of a garbage bag
Burning my lungs with a special soft pack
Who will live and who will die
Who will flip a page in my own mag
And your hunger and junker taunting you to have a tan tang
Retire the crown
You'll never drown
And let her touch
And you will see
She's the latest
Most greatest
Curley Faces

It's Wednesday and the markets are open. Five timely things to note this morning:

Robbers use their time most efficiently than anybody else.

Lessons from times past of self-mistakes have inestimable values compared to those from someone else's teachings.

There is an opaque line drawn between living in denial and having faith; one that contrarily blurs their distinction over time rather than sharply divides them.

If eight-in-ten people were to live on for millennia (in granted impeccable health and comfort), they would witness firsthand how time immemorial of overzealous passion to divinity had nothing to do with spirituality, and concede to the other two it was all emotionally charged quasi-adolescent fabrications that lingered on for far too long.

Time does tell, when you give it time.

You classify, and judge and you justify. Then you've lost interest for a period and nothing will bring you back because by the time it's realized you're far-gone and it's a statistic. Goddamn I thought it was special. And just because almost everyone is pretty much the same does not mean they're the norm. It's 12/21/12 as it's coming and will be going like any other tomorrow that became yesterday.

If there were one thing to look forward to, it'd be enough.

You can blame you for me.
You can't blame me for me.
Only me can blame me for me.

Created a monster
Living secretly among us
Who w/ great power
Could create giant balls of
SOUND of SAND
To drop & spread
Filling a little girl's
Hair w/ fine
Grains on a darkened
Beach but leaving
No harmony _____

Cold sidewalk you make my life so blue
You're dirty and dark and I hate every inch of you
You're hard on my bare feet
You suck my dignity
If I only had my past powers
I'd jackhammer you to Berkeley

Happy people pass by and come and go
They look me down like a worthless John Doe
They laugh and hold hands
I think about my old homelands
And you sidewalk make me feel so low

You're covered with dog feces and urine
And the mucosal spit of businessmen
I sit amid and wonder if I'm still human
Cold sidewalk I really really hate you
Even chimps have it better at the zoo
San Francisco sidewalk I lost to you

He planned
One last desolate
Night to himself
And wasn't prepared
To give it away
He stopped to wonder
About two past friends
What'd done
Why went astray
It was the eccentric hero
And a friend Hilda'd chased
While screaming in high heels
As Fitzgerald shouted
"Get outa heah!"
As she cried
"You don't know how it feels!"
They spoke
Of Rider Haggard's adventures
How Hilda was so stern
In her final year
And when he got up
To bid her good night
He walked out
Into a morning sun so clear
She begged and pleaded
"If you would," for him
She said, she could
Leave it all behind
He knew it was crazy
He named her Daisy
And sang her "Winterlude"
Every night.

friends don't let friends remain friends

The Dead of tomorrow
Gather together in a room
Conform to their habit
I spectate & join
At once

May you fulfill all your hopes, and may all your wishes come true. May you never wonder what it all came to, or why you often feel so blue. May you not realize that everything you thought forever is now no longer possible whatsoever.

It's Wednesday, allegedly halving the week, and if you today don't know why you do half or most of what you do most or half of the week, that's because nobody knows anything all week, but so long as you rid yourself of expectations, you and everyone may emerge content with all you, and everyone, do all week.

We buried our cousin
We shook hands
And all of a sudden
We were cousins again

There are too many. But to answer that one question about why I need your mentorship is because you go off on tangents.

If you talk to me
It'd better be
Past eighteen O one
Because everything prior
Has already been done

Woman down the hall
Careful of that man's call
Nothing will stop him
Until you give it all
His world is dying, your stance is defying
And that man after you is just horrifying

Only as a sop I said, "you did what you did and I do what I do." As I shrugged my shoulders, "and those who actually get it are so few," as he shook his head, turned away and said my younger self, "I hate you, too."

To the stumblers and stragglers; it's October 5th in San Francisco. If yesterday's American Swamp Rock is celestial, Tony Joe White is a galaxy. Meanwhile, the Sun is doing its own thing and there's nothing you can do about it.

Not. At all. I laugh at he, I laugh at me, and I laugh at thee. Not at all.

We were complementary. I mean, to each other. Like, we mixed well together. A little bit of she, a little bit of me. You should have seen us; it was the only type of complimentary you'd want to pay to see. Neither one demanded, nor deserved. We were meeting for a moment, mutually content, complementing each other.

A broken soul
Lives at my door
It's dark out here
Horripilation of fear
Owl's whisper flight
Rise, shine my dear

I'm forever flattered by you taking interest in me. And I thank you for appearing on my own TV.

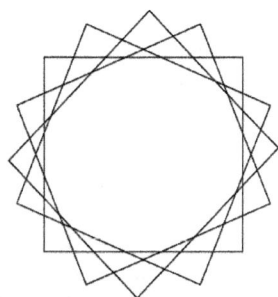

Good morning.

- Good morning.

Underestimated is the pent-up exertion of the nondestructive nihilist.

- Superbly invincible is the apathetic.

Good mourning.

- Good mourning.

Now tell me here you fancy autodidact, what did you teach yourself today?

- I do shit I don't like to do so I can do shit I like to do.

And what did you learn from that?

- It's all shit.

- How late?

Pretty late.

- How late is pretty late?

Usually ten years to any date.

- That's pretty damn late.

Time is a sharp heavy weight. Is it worth fighting oneself for?

- One always ends up lonely…ain't no use in war to end war.

And One isn't the loneliest number if you count no more.

- Were there patterns on her tight skirt?

Yes, black on white.

- Tall blonde?

Maybe... it was late at night.

- Did she discuss how Cairo is crying? Cairo is dying?

Yes, but that it would be reborn.

- And did she mourn, the misguided voting right?

Yes, and for the idealistic playwrights whose morals are collided and judge those just like them while their agendas are confided.

- Ok Ok, that's quite alright.

Actually it ain't right. No one's to judge whether the skirt is tight.

He was carrying a weapon.
He threatened me with it.
I was scared for my life.
I want to speak with my attorney.

- *A watch is not a weapon.*

He pointed at the time!

Dark brows, gypsy curls, long and autumn brown.

- And the nose ring.

Them ear hoops too.

- And those diplomas on the wall.

And the courage to fend for oneself too.

- Any government, culture, religion, or tradition that suppresses women in any form whatsoever, is forever miserable, hopeless, and inherently impaired, where peace, harmony, or progress is nonexistent, and poisonous failure is the only consistent outcome of such convoluted oppression.

A good man is a rare exception.

How long does one keep on going like this before he's shown the way, or shown the way out?

- *The way out to one is more of an end rather than a place like it is to some.*

A place to some is additional time of similar chronology with a different outcome, but to others it's only an imagination.

- *Imaginations that are externally triggered by a blue sky, sound of waves, heavy rain. . . etc., are far more relevant than those internally triggered (i.e. voices in head that make one write).*

If a Writer becomes so good by keeping busy penning down his ideas and wins awards for them, doesn't the Reader deserve more awards because she's the one who thinks more of what the writings are all about?

- *Didn't someone write something about those who are delusional in life; those who absolutely believe deep within themselves that they are far better off by many folds when comparing themselves to those just like them exactly?*

I'm having such a time. I crawled so far back in my mind.

- *Obnoxious players don't get a voice. Do you want mine?*

No, and don't mistake a laugh for a friendly smile.

- *Wake up man. Geniwine is often misspelled.*

So be it. And so y'all be expelled.

- How far?

Not that far.

- How far is not that far?

To the girl at end of the bar.

- One from Tiananmen Square?

One from Tahrir Square.

- Sigh... they all just remind me of Myanmar.

"All"?! ummm... uhhh... errr!

- Have you heard of this grownup man who's timid like a declawed tabby cat?

And temperamental like a blind Tasmanian tiger, the chronic malcontent drama monger?

- Yes!

He lives only to survive non-submersibley, evades all commitments obstinately, and approaches everything so hesitantly?

- Yes!

Who motivates himself only to desert it after misguided loquacious reasoning, has grown absorbed in daydreaming, the only safe place for such a weakling?

- Yes!

The man whose every living thought ceases with a desperate longing to strike anew, as he neglects to live the present only to reminisce about it sadly in rear view?

- Yes!

The man whose logic is of eristic mendacious remarks about dismal self, and carries no zeal besides emotional hypochondriac nonsense?

- Yes!

Whose only effective sanity-saving remedy is to make art, yet doesn't even try to start, might as well be a dilettante?

- Yes!

No, actually I've never heard of such man.

- Melancholia is of the quintessential narcissist. I say wake the fuck up. Shake it the fuck out. Look around. There is a lot more than just you.

You are the most ignorant, insensible and oblivious blathering fool; there is no ego, nor self-interest. On the contrary, asshole.

- How's daytime TV, Bob?

Well now I have to get a day job.

- It's that bad, daytime TV, Bob?

Well not quite daytime TV per se, it's just that daytime is so blasé.

Um... I don't know. A gun comes to mind.

- Gee! I was thinking more like a... pillow.

Everything I say is a lie.

- I love myself more than anyone else and I hate myself for that I wish I didn't have to love it back.

Nothing I say is a lie.

- Today I saw beautiful seagulls fighting over a slice of pizza.

Some I say is a lie.

- It's moments like this when I want to exercise my summon privileges.

Some I say is not a lie.

And are you excited; what do you say?

- Man, it couldn't happen any sooner I say.

That's not a nice thing to say. I don't think that's what you meant to say.

- When you're a poetaster, you say what you want to say.

Ainot. Ainot. Ainot.

- Something is possibly right.

It's never been more right. The only problem with that is: is right right?

A mutual friend?

- Close. How about a mute friend?

Why?

- *Look at me. I'm paddling only to stay afloat. I don't want to paddle to stay afloat. I don't even want to worry about being afloat. I look around and see flying birds with wings, swimming fish with gills, and men and women sleeping on boats. I don't want to keep paddling to only stay afloat. I'd rather sink and grow gills or fly high in ease on wings yet I find bodies filled with bisphinol-a and no one cares but questions remain about how a cancer salad infused with ulcers come about. Was it the kickshaw I inhaled and ingested and consumed with illusive regard and disrespect at my life's expense as I cloistered myself in mainstream existence only to end up befriending hospital misfits?*

(And I said nothing to that.)

You've got to do something. Maybe it's not what you want, but at the end, it's what you do get done.

- And I do wonder about that something. That's something I get done.

- Has the perfect incident ever occur?

As a matter of fact, yes.

- And what would a lame lacker say?

Well, something like:

> "Sorry I did not get a chance to say goodbye. Sorry I had nothing to say while you were there. Your friends' voices in the distance seemed like the rip current that sucked you away. Sorry I could not rescue you. Or me. Goodbye."

- Yeah. Lame Lacker.

Those who are bitter until the second they die are truly human.

- How so?

They are pissed off throughout it all and remain so until the end.

- How so?

Ever notice how people become nicer as they get older, as if being nicer helps them hang on to life a little bit longer?

- How so?

Well those rare nice old ones pretend to be so as if to deny the inevitable in a desperate attempt to cope with what lies ahead. Those who are bitter until the second they die are truly human.

- Not so.

The Blinding Blonde!

- *What she sing?*

Brain Chunks on The Tile.

Time?

- *Savor it doing something. Pass it trying to be someone. Waste it thinking about it.*

Relax bro, I mean what's the time?

- *3:19... and wasted.*

What if the only one you really know does not really know you?

- hmm… I don't really know.

- Which side are you on?

US and them.

- Which side are you really on?

US not them.

How exceptionally ingenious the word "year" is may lie in how pleasant it sounds. It isn't its origin but it must have something to do with "yearning" - to want, desire and long for what lies ahead in the future. Imagine if the word were better representative of what it actually means in the context of time, like "malformedshitter". Any honest work could take a whole malformedshitter to complete. January would bring a new malformedshitter all over again. Every birthday you would be celebrating another malformedshitter.

- You celebrate?

- How many of you?

One of Two.

- Not true. More or none.

Ok. Two of One.

- No that's still a few.

Then everything under the Sun.

- Do you even know which one, or who's who?

I try but all breaks undone, then I start anew.

It is my opinion that he was a nihilist, a pessimist, a reasonable one.

- *Was?*

- Five is the new Four because of this girl dead center.

Mmmm. The Blinding Blonde. What a taste. What a taste. In music and on canvas.

- When are you going to finally admit that you are such a procrastinator?!

I'll do it tomorrow.

Oooh that thin line outline.

- That fine line you can't cross?

That one around the thumbnail.

- One raised by a look-alike Betty Ross?

One on a yakking Nebraskan bronze.

- It's 1978. We will be having the age talk now.

What?!! Fuck this shit damn cock sucker motherfucker bullshit ass son of a fucking bitch piss this shit what the fuck I just got here for shit sakes damn the fucking sucking bullshit!

Here is a dollar. Go buy yourself something.

Hey, how much is this?

- *Seventy-five cents.*

Hmm ok.. how much is this?

- *Eighty-nine cents.*

How about this?

- *Sixty cents.*

Um.. do you have anything for a dollar?

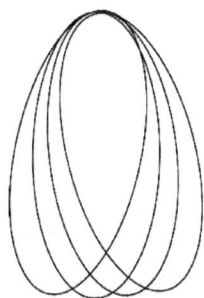

First of all I'd like to say thanks a lot
To my muse by whom I turned a sot

She like everyone believes in life at the womb
I nurse and shed my stiff in a dark cordial tomb

Sacrosanct poems are as heavy as moraines
Carried down the years of our infinite ravine

Trust not to sleep or sorrow
She would croon, She would lull

Thank you O Girl for your vaguish sleep
Your city was built upon a garbage heap

"Hi"
"*Hello*" he says.

She's married with two children.
He's harried.

They take up photography.

Many a love note's been written, and this is one of them:

Come tell me all about your pink night in Cattolica
Come on you leave Munich to Barcelona to Marbella
Come back to San Francisco for homemade sangria
Your California soul's gotten mine brighter
You're my lamp, my lifeboat, my ladder

In Anaheim... im. im. immm. In a large bright studio where there are only the two of us. I'm shy and you're reserved. Your long black hair disappears into your black ensemble and your soft white skin glistens with the sun light through the windows. I smile and you do too. I'm transfixed. You say it's all long work and wish more could fit in four hours, as the brush in your hand strokes your melliferous canvas and your smile grows bigger. I open up and all barriers suddenly disappear into your voice of reason. Your friends don't give me a chance and I bid you farewell when a dog bites my hand and I bleed out through a rubber glove. At the hospital, two young women and a man in white coats are occupied with gossip over medical supplies, yet I can't get you out of my head. I stare at the sky and reminisce about our time at the studio. Your magic is my source of dying; how come you love me?

The only reason why I walk where I do
Is because I think one day I might run into you
I walk in circles like O

The dream we were in came and went, just like in the real our moments flee. Your soft whispers I still hear. I was excited to frame your work's print and your smile grew adoringly big, that was when I probably came off too glib. I was just reeled in by your hypnotic stare and got lost in your long wavy hair. You may not read this or even care, and I know it was just a dream, yet felt overwhelmed, then compelled, to promise to be forever true to you. Suddenly a friend showed up, you walked off, I thought that sucked, then I balked, and woke up. I obviously love you; that's my dream's clou and nub.

If you act scared when I run into you, it's ok because I know you know what I had been up to back when it used to be all about you.

Many a love note's been written, and this is one of them:

You visited softly in a dream
Embodying all girls of my dreams
With such tender spirit
My heart awoke agleam
A ritual, muse, bloom
The moon
Don't shine for you
I do

This girl you like and the first car you owned.
Together, in the same dream.
Why would one ever want to wake up?

Cruelty at its core.

One Heart
One One / One One / One One
This is to all the singles
And to the One in Wilde's one

As I pull on my chin's hair (that's my beard)
Screaming for the Giants, that team so revered
Do you really plan on going home alone
Do you really think you can catch the ball
If I come, will you give me your all
Baby, why you so rigid
Girl, I mean, come on

It was the last quarter of the moon
We smoked in darkness off of a bent spoon
She reached my lineage secret too soon
Then everything went "BOOM! BOOM!"

Many a love note's been written, and this is one of them:

Did you enjoy Tokyo and Seoul
Did they adorn your heart with joy
I can't take you to Korea nor Japan
Never to Leeds or even Cannes
One thing I can do is holdout
I'll wait
I'm hopelessly devout

She's an Egyptian Olivian rockin my world
I told her say good bye but that wouldn't fly
Got her on the telephone painting me peace signs
I look and smile man she's rockin my world

She's an Egyptian Olivian rockin my world
I told her say good bye but that wouldn't fly
Saw her just last night giving me them looks
I musta been dreamin she's rockin my world

She's an Egyptian Olivian rockin my world
I told her say good bye but that was a lie
Now she's right next to me breathin on my shoulder
All I have ever wanted she's rockin my world

If there were only just one image one gets to keep with his last roars I'd want mine to be one of yours shyly looking at me directly into my lens with your brush against your canvas and your freckles on your chest beaming glorious tender marks of beautiful, beautiful bliss nothing more, nothing less only this image of you for me to suggest that one of them days I might've been your guest as I close my eyes and reminisce how I was forever impressed by your bristles' artful and tender caress.

She's a cocktail server, not a bartender
Comes and goes to please ma drinker

She deserves her own dais
I don't care what anyone says
And to quote just one phrase
"These visions of Johanna
Have now taken my place."

Many a love note's been written, and this is one of them:

When Miami is lucky to have you for a warm late autumn's week
And you stroll through convention booths in white and bare feet
And your manager and dealer hail and marvel at your each story
And you're pulled in to chat it up with Greg Gossel and Brett Amory
My head and heart and abdomen hurt and it's not even the sorbitol
It's just that I miss you and life without you is nothing but folderol

My only grief with this is that even though you say you don't know I know you know I called you up ten years ago and left you a message and you called me back and left me a message then I called you back but you said you were mixing drinks and busy answering fan letters and you'd call me back but your friend called and said "she ain't the one" and I dropped my cigarette on the ground and ever since I've always wondered if I had lost my one chance and now I replay your message and remember you through this recall afraid to breathe in for it might not come out and hoping to ease a ten-year repentance through a run-on sentence.

Last night I wrote you off to the hurricane
Woke up today to the warmest sunshine
Now I celebrate with OJ and Champagne
For a minute there thought you were mine
But I take comfort I'll never see you again
And already hardly remember your name

The moment I left you
The nightmares stopped
How dare you judge me now
After all you've robbed
Mistakes are for the ballsy
With which our bond's fraught
No way will you do this now
So long you false formidable

Separation anxiety is such a drag.

Many a love note's been written, and this is one of them:

It's almost June again and I try yet can't help but reminisce
That late night at your studio when it was just the two of us
Açai for breakfast then drove from Oakland to Los Angeles

It's ok now
The only thing we had in common was you
I'm ok too
I don't really hate it (actually that's not true)

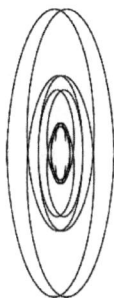

I have an answer to each of your questions; none to mine.

I'm only a number to you, and so are you to me. You don't know me, neither can you even say my name. You and I are only a number to the rest of us, too.

Those who wish for fewer rats in the morning are greedy rats themselves. And those with repetitive coward dreams of the dawning are witnesses of Complacency's marriage to Incompetence. The production of Sloth that twins Comfort is observed by the complainer while yawning, who puts forth attempts to mainstream's dissolution, only to reaffirm the inherited constitution. The rat race is what it all is and a wonderful soul seeks no more.

When morals first collide with one's will, it signals the beginning of the end to oneself's morals, or the oneself altogether. The observation is that will and morals (generally those based on deferred rewards, and specifically those of modern religion) cannot coexist in conflict for long; it's the classic unstoppable force against an immovable object. At least they appear as such at the beginning until one cedes to the other, which happens often in my opinion.

It bothers me a great deal when people judge one another by their own standards, yet I find it unsurprisingly common and quite expected. "Comeuppance" is also one that bothers me. The word implies that the sayer knows what one's fate is, and is something which one deserves. Not a single being knows what one's fate is because it is inherently something that's outside of any person's control. The sayer falsely claims prior knowledge of such fate and simultaneously reinforces the retribution it brings. The sound of the word itself is also pretty terrible. An escape through semantic satiation won't even work.

I admire and pity the position of the man who is second-in-command; he has to make up for the absurdities his chief has foolishly caused by maintaining incredible self-restrain against his own will and experimental desires in fear of baring additional absurdities onto the clan.

I wonder whether those who perpetually fall in love aren't seeking the thing of itself but the *falling in* is what they're feening for. Perhaps the repetition is due to the lack of romance in the love they come to find, whereas they learn it's the *falling in* that has it all. Or maybe it's neither of the two, and is only a mere proximity infatuation, which I find is more common and usually confused with admiration and the feelings of falling in love, accentuated by the emotional rush of inceptive romance. Now while the true motivation behind each form is debatable, a definite conclusion can be made; the fleeting nature is a common attribute among them all, and everything else beyond that, too.

Morals are the rules made up by the scared to institute boundaries against one's natural will. Because a natural will is not something to reason with, particularly at its strongest, a weak society must firmly apply a form of faith-based rule to contain such strong will since both are of virtual substance (i.e. fight fire with fire).

Aphorisms almost always bring about emotional reactions. Why is because I believe the observer already has such insight within them, but cannot articulate it not even to one's own self. The observer needs only the confirmation to their rooted intentions to unearth what's already there, and use such to serve as the emotion's last push-off the edge into reaction. Such reach comes from the gnomist's primeval talent with pithy phrases. My observation then is that at least two people think of the same thing, only one says it better than the other. For example, "we're all a product of pleasure" and at least one other person, perhaps you, thought of it already. My other observation also finds that the aphorisms that ignite strongest emotions of deepest levels are the kind that is quoted to some "Anonymous" perhaps because the observer imagines themselves as the writer with the apparent lack of a definite source. The observer is able to digest it neutrally because they cannot judge the origin without a referenced name (that first source of stereotyping). The observer takes it for what it is and is moved. "Death is life, only without you" is quoted by Anonymous and is brilliant and inflames humility, and I feel like it belongs to me. Or, Krause Obengaard said that, and it's prolific, but also hints at 19th century Western philosophy, bordering nihilism, a category misunderstood by many, yet either way categorizing now has me instead. Or, Shiek Farzoud Nagbi wrote that, which warrants questioning into his current whereabouts and the background of his recent contemporaries. This is also an emotional reaction to the aphorism, albeit by the authorities in this case.

There is this assumption that free will produces good will; there is also the assumption when the majority approves *some* will, it's proclaimed *the* good will. Neither will prove true in my opinion for as long as truth is known to me. Just imagine a world without accountability and ramifications. Imagine yourself at sixteen and the parents are away for a week. The dishes are the last thing you think to do with the masses you invite over.

You are who you are more often than when you are not. And how you come across has something to do with how you see yourself. Do not let those around you shape or make you forget yourself. Keep going back to who you are because you are more than you are not.

Why there is so little learned from past times when it comes to wrongfully resolving conflict with violence is perhaps because violence is the human's second nature, for a human is merely an animal, but in this sense, a cruel one who inflicts pain on another for no primary reason other than causing incredible physical harm as revenge or to prove a point. I see that we still tend to deal with it today with the kind of aggressive finger-on-the-trigger immediacy that very much resembles the dawn of conflict with Sumer and Elam; "I will kill you and everyone you know to show that killing people is wrong." I can't separate myself and judge it however. As a human, personally, if a cab honks at me, I'm compulsively honking right back, particularly if I think I have a louder horn, whether I'm in the right is irrelevant. It is my observation, which is to say that of all the kinds of violent nature in this world, a human's violence is the toughest to expunge, if at all possible.

If we had no challenges to labor through, particularly those that are virtual (like morals), we would either die from boredom or become invincible, omnipotent, to whom barriers are nonexistent. Neither scenario depicts our nature; therefore, manmade challenges are as natural as sunlight as all other.

When two men have a conflict then bring you in and plead for your opinion, beware because either one may only be interested in you to win him a majority rather than hear your actual opinion.

At most, you'd probably get a documentary here and there, maybe in three languages (one of them in subtitles, which won't count), a two-page article in circulation every third odd year, and a random reference by a twenty-some in dark shades and a helmet under his arm. And once in a blue moon you may experience resurgence along with a Friday night special on some TV network. Your chances are one in seven billion, unless you drop a title or two of some contemporary science books, particularly those about quantum physics or a reference to string theory (the introduction of the topic alone could suffice since most conversations of such subject are only long enough for someone to quickly sense the aplomb and move on). You'll wing it alright.

I think the worst one of all is to be upset with yourself, because you continue to live with it for there is not even temporary separation to help cope with its mistakes, nor permanent abandonment to avoid future ones. There is punishment, but it would be of weak reasoning and misguided emotions to judge yourself and act retaliatorily against it, too. That's just unfair, particularly to your younger self. It just didn't know what you now do. And that younger self includes you seconds ago, too, which also means you shouldn't be upset with yourself about the time you spent reading this if you learned nothing at all. You just didn't know what you now do.

There are those who get it, and those who don't, and in between is everybody else, the automatons, who are just like "meh..."